James H. & Michele D.
Unger

1st Anniversary
February 27th, 1994

G.FVMAGALLI

# A Vow of Love

Andrews and McMeel
A Universal Press Syndicate Company
Kansas City

ISBN: 0-8362-7992-1
Library of Congress Catalog Number: XX-XXXXX

Printed in Singapore
First U.S. edition
1  3  5  7  9  10  8  6  4  2

Edited by Linda Sunshine
Designed by Dirk Kaufman
Produced by Smallwood and Stewart, Inc.
New York City

Credits and copyright notices appear on page 95.

# Introduction

hroughout the ages, poets and writers have celebrated the vows of love we bestow ~ from youth's first, tender declaration of devotion to the most enduring of relationships. Thus, this collection pays tribute to the full spectrum of love's evolution ~ young love, first meetings, marriage proposals, wedding celebrations, married love, and lifelong commitments. Shakespeare, who always found the most perfect words to express human emotions, once wrote that love is "an ever-fixed mark . . . the star to every wandering bark, whose worth's unknown, although his height be taken."

Indeed, love is life's most profound inspiration and source of wonderment, constantly changing and yet remaining ever timeless. "Love is all we have," wrote Euripides sometime around 420 B.C., a sentiment that would be voiced similarly over two thousand years later in *All You Need Is Love*, a Beatles song. It is perhaps no wonder then that, though the nuances of love may vary, we are endlessly fascinated by it and its countless forms of expression.

As ever, we turn to the great literary geniuses when our own lives are filled with thoughts of love. And how familiar those words seem to us! Johann Wolfgang von Goethe declared that "we are shaped and fashioned by what we love." In one of his many letters to Fanny Brawne, John Keats wrote, "My creed is love and you are its only tenet." And the poet, Alfred, Lord Tennyson, proclaimed: "Brief is life but long is love."

Such poignant remarks touch us in many ways, just as love itself touches and ultimately transforms our lives. May the sentiments expressed in this volume serve to enhance and enlighten your own personal vows of love.

*But there's nothing half so sweet in life*

*As love's young dream.*

Clement C. Moore

*I*n our orchard I saw you picking dewy apples with your mother (I was showing you the way). I had just turned twelve years old, I could reach the brittle branches even from the ground: how I saw you! how I fell in love! how an awful madness swept me away!

*Virgil,* Ecologue

. . . I was at a party feeling very shy because there were a lot of celebrities around, and I was sitting in a corner alone and a very beautiful young man came up to me and offered me some salted peanuts and he said, "I wish they were emeralds" as he handed me the peanuts and that was the end of my heart.

I never got it back.

*Helen Hayes on first meeting her husband,*
*Charles MacArthur*

. . . she was like the girl in the fairy story whose

words turned to pearls as they fell from her lips.

*L. P. Hartley,* The Go-Between

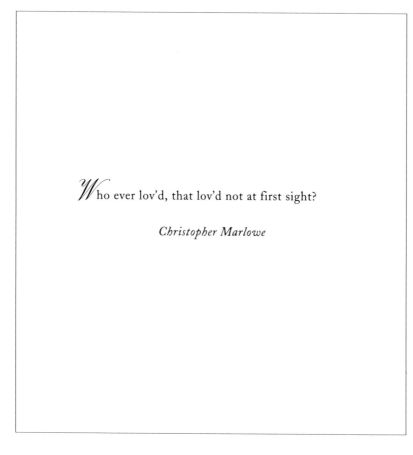

Who ever lov'd, that lov'd not at first sight?

*Christopher Marlowe*

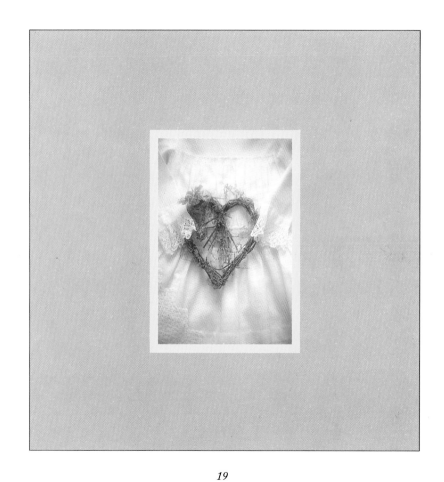

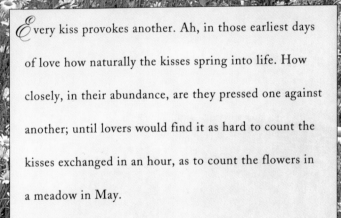

*E*very kiss provokes another. Ah, in those earliest days of love how naturally the kisses spring into life. How closely, in their abundance, are they pressed one against another; until lovers would find it as hard to count the kisses exchanged in an hour, as to count the flowers in a meadow in May.

*Marcel Proust*, Swann's Way

"*L*ove," she said, "seems to pump me full of vitamins. It makes me feel as if the sun were shining and my hat was right and my shoes were right and my frock was right and my stockings were right, and somebody just left me ten thousand a year."

*P. G. Wodehouse,* Spring Fever

We always believe our first love is our last,
and our last love our first.

*George Whyte-Melville*

*Love is anterior to life,*

*Posterior to death,*

*Initial of creation, and*

*The exponent of breath.*

Emily Dickinson

*O*ne word frees us of all the weight and pain of life: That word is love.

*Sophocles*, Oedipus at Colonus

*L*ove is a canvas furnished by nature and embroidered by imagination.

*Voltaire*

*L*ove is all we have, the only way that each can help the other.

*Euripides*, Orestes

*W*here love is concerned, too much is not even enough.

*Pierre-Augustin de Beaumarchais,* The Marriage of Figaro

*l*overs alone wear sunlight

*e. e. cummings*

*L*ove is but the discovery of ourselves in others, and
the delight in the recognition.

*Alexander Smith,* Dreamthorp

*Love one another, but make not a bond of love:*

*Let it rather be a moving sea between the shores of your souls.*

*Fill each other's cup but drink not from one cup.*

*Give one another of your bread but eat not from the same loaf.*

Kahlil Gibran, *The Prophet*

"I mean that I love you," he said quietly. "You can keep the knowledge, if you care to and it means anything to you. I didn't intend to tell you, but I am told that women like the thought of hopeless love; the more the merrier, perhaps. A little trophy for you, something to hang on your bracelet ~ like this!" He took off his signet-ring, kissed it and put it into her hand. "When you are an old lady, you can show it to your grand-children, and say 'That one was Esmé's ~ or was it Tom's, or Dick's or Harry's?' Never mind, it will all be forgotten, except that I told you my love when I meant not to, and you had that triumph ~ meagre as it was against all the others."

She put one palm over the other, the ring safe between them, and wondered what to say. She wanted to clutch at some of his words before they faded, but already they were flying away from her. . . . "I haven't thanked you. For the ring, I mean, and for what you said. No words will come. All I can say is that I love you, too, and have for years and shall for ever. "

*Elizabeth Taylor*, Angel

*A* kiss can be a comma, a question mark or an exclamation point. That's basic spelling that every woman ought to know.

*Mistinguette*

"It is this, that ever since I have seen you, I know not why, you have taken a place in my life; that, if I drive the thought of you out of my mind, it always comes back; that when I met you to-day, after not having seen you for two years, you made a deeper impression on my heart and mind than ever; that, now that you have let me come to see you, now that I know you, now that I know all that is strange in you, you have become a necessity of my life, and you will drive me mad, not only if you will not love me, but if you will not let me love you."

*Alexandre Dumas fils*, Camille

No love, no friendship

can cross the path of our

destiny without leaving

some mark on it forever.

*François Mauriac*

The supreme happiness

of life is the conviction

that we are loved.

*Victor Hugo*

$\mathcal{T}$here is only one situation I can think of in which men and women make an effort to read better than they usually do. When they are in love and reading a love letter, they read for all they are worth. They read every word three ways; they read between the lines and in the margins. . . They may even take the punctuation into account. Then, if never before or after, they read.

*Mortimer J. Adler,* Quote *magazine*

## WONDERFUL BOY,

Where are you tonight? Your letter came only an hour ago ~ cruel hour ~ I had hope you would spend it with me here.

Paris is a morgue without you: before I knew you, it was Paris, and I thought it was heaven; but now it is a vast desert of desolation and loneliness. It is like the face of a clock, bereft of its hands.

All the pictures that hung in my memory before I knew you have faded and given place to our radiant moments together.

Now I cannot live apart from you ~ your words, even though bitter ~ dispel all the cares of the world and make me happy; my art has been suckled by them and softly rocked in their tender cradle; they are as necessary to me now as sunlight and air.

I am as hungry for them as for food. I am thirsty for them, and my thirst is overwhelming. Your words are my food, your breath my wine. You are everything to me.

Your Sarah

*letter from Sarah Bernhardt to Victorien Sardou*

. . . And suddenly I realised that it would all

happen, I would be his wife, we would walk

in the garden together, we would stroll down

that path in the valley to the shingle beach.

I knew how I would stand on the steps after

breakfast, looking at the day, throwing crumbs

to the birds, and later wander out in a shady

hat with long scissors in my hand, and cut

flowers for the house.

*Daphne du Maurier,* Rebecca

Safe for the minute, sealed down under her eyelids, Portia lay and saw herself with Eddie. She saw a continent in the late sunset, in rolls and ridges of shadow like the sea. Light that was dark yellow lay on trees, and penetrated their dark hearts. Like a struck glass, the continent rang with silence. The country, with its slow tense dusk-drowned ripple, rose to their feet where they sat: she and Eddie sat in the door of a hut. She felt the hut, with its content of dark, behind them. The unearthly level light streamed in their faces; she saw it touch his cheekbones, the tips of his eyelashes, while he turned her way his eyeballs blind with gold. She saw his hands hanging down between his knees, and her hands hanging down peacefully beside him as they sat together on the step of the hut. She felt the touch of calmness and similarity: he and she were one without any touch but this. What was in the hut behind her she did not know: this light was eternal; they would be here for ever.

*Elizabeth Bowen*, The Death of the Heart

Nevertheless, I am in a dream, a flustered, happy, hurried dream. I can't believe that it is going to be; and yet I can't believe but that every one I pass in the street, must have some kind of perception, that I am to be married the day after tomorrow.

*Charles Dickens,* David Copperfield

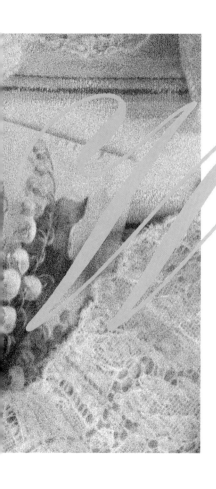

*ith this ring I thee wed,*
*with my body I thee worship,*
*and with my worldly goods I thee endow.*

Book of Common Prayer

The June roses over the porch were awake bright and early on that morning. Meg looked very like a rose herself. Neither silk, lace, nor orange flowers would she have. "I don't want to look strange or fixed up today," she said. "I don't want a fashionable wedding but only those about me whom I love, and to them I wish to look and be my familiar self."

So she made her wedding gown herself. Her sisters braided her pretty hair, and the only ornaments she wore were the lilies of the valley which John liked best of all the flowers that grew. . . .

There was no bridal procession, but a sudden silence fell on the room as Mr. March and the young pair took their places under the green arch. Mother  and sisters gathered close, the fatherly voice broke more than once, which only seemed to make the service more beautiful and solemn. The bridegroom's hand trembled visibly and no one heard his replies, but Meg looked straight up into her husband's eyes and said, "I will!" with such tender trust in her own face and voice that Aunt March sniffed audibly.

*Louisa May Alcott,* Little Women

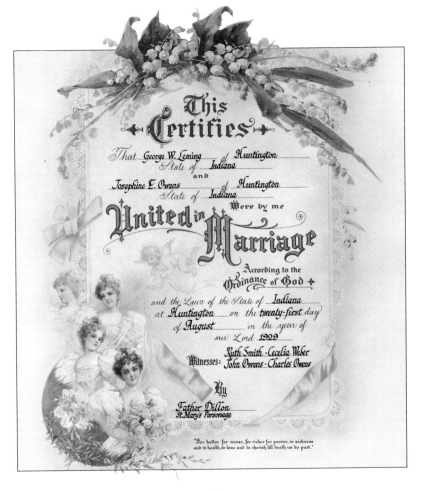

This
◆ Certifies ◆

That _George W. Leming_ of _Huntington_
State of _Indiana_
and
_Josephine E. Owens_ of _Huntington_
State of _Indiana_
Were by me

United in Marriage

According to the
◆ Ordinance of God ◆

and the Laws of the State of _Indiana_
at _Huntington_ on the _twenty-first_ day
of _August_ in the year of
our Lord _1929_

Witnesses: _Ruth Smith · Cecelia Weber_
_John Owens · Charles Owens_

By

_Father Dillon_
St. Mary's Parsonage

"For better for worse, for richer for poorer, in sickness
and in health, to love and to cherish till death us do part."

54

*L*ove that has been given to you is
too sacred a thing to be talked of to
anyone . . . except just to the person
who is like part of you and who will
feel it as you do.

*Olive Schreiner,*
Letters of Olive Schreiner

# Marriages are made in Heaven

*Alfred, Lord Tennyson*, Aylmer's Field

We were married by the mayor of the small village where my mother lived. I wore a white dress printed with red strawberries, the children were dressed in a matching red pattern and Paolo sported a red silk tie. In all the photographs I have, we are smiling at one another, and we look happy. . . . For our wedding lunch we went by boat to the small island of Burano, where the famous fish restaurant 'da Romano' had prepared a glorious feast of delicacies from the lagoon.

Wind in our hair, smell of seaweed, screams of seagulls, and the island fading like a mirage in the wake of the boats. . . .

The following day, with Paolo's daughters and my son, and a great deal of luggage, we took off from Venice airport, bound for Africa and our new life.

*Kuki Gallmann*, I Dreamed of Africa

happy marriage has in it all the pleasures of
friendships, all the enjoyments of sense and reason ~
and indeed all the sweets of life.

*Joseph Addison,* The Spectator *magazine*

Everyone has attended a wedding ball at least once in his life, and can hardly fail to smile as he recalls all those weddings guests in their Sunday best with expressions to match. . . . There they all are, as one remembers them, rich and poor, envious and envied, the cynics and the dazzled dreamers, all clustered like the flowers in a bouquet around one rare flower, the bride. A wedding ball is a miniature world.

*Honoré de Balzac*, Cousin Bette

A good marriage is that in which each appoints the other guardian of his solitude. Once the realization is accepted that even between the closest human beings infinite distances continue to exist, a wonderful living side by side can grow up, if they succeed in loving the distance between them which makes it possible for each to see the other whole and against a wide sky.

*Rainer Maria Rilke,* Letters

*He carried her to the window,*

so that she, too, saw the view. They sank upon their knees,
invisible from the road, they hoped, and began to whisper
one another's names. Ah! it was worth while; it was the
great joy that they had expected, and countless little joys
of which they had never dreamt. . . .

Then they spoke of other things ~ the desultory talk
of those who have been fighting to reach one another, and
whose reward is to rest quietly in each other's arms.

*E. M. Forster,* A Room with a View

*How many loved your moments of glad grace,*

*And loved your beauty with love false or true,*

*But one man loved the pilgrim soul in you,*

*And loved the sorrows of your changing face.*

W.B. Yeats, *The Countess Kathleen*

## SONNET CXV

*Those lines that I before have writ, do lie;*

*Even those that said I could not love you dearer;*

*Yet then my judgment knew no reason why*

*My most full flame should afterwards burn clearer.*

*But reckoning time, whose million'd accidents*

*Creep in 'twixt vows, and change decrees of kings,*

*Tan sacred beauty, blunt the sharp'st intents,*

*Divert strong minds to the course of altering things;*

*Alas! why, fearing of Time's tyranny,*

*Might I not then say, 'Now I love you best,'*

*When I was certain o'er incertainty,*

*Crowning the present, doubting of the rest?*

> *Love is a babe; then might I not say so,*

> *To give full growth to that which still doth grow?*

William Shakespeare

*If ever two were one, then surely we.*

*If ever man were loved by wife, then thee.*

Anne Bradstreet,
*To My Dear and Loving Husband*

After a youth and manhood passed half in unutterable

misery and half in dreary solitude, I have for the first time

found what I can truly love ~ I have found *you*. You are my

sympathy ~ my better self ~ my good angel ~ I am bound

to you with a strong attachment. I think you good, gifted,

lovely: a fervent, a solemn passion is conceived in my

heart; it leans to you, draws you to my centre and spring

of life, wraps my existence about you ~ and, kindling in

pure, powerful flame, fuses you and me in one.

*Charlotte Brontë*, Jane Eyre

There is no more lovely, friendly and charming relationship,

communion or company than a good marriage.

*Martin Luther,* Table Talk

The very intimacy to which she admitted him, her tenderness for him, confirmed him in this state of mind. No other woman had been tender to Charlie Allnutt. . . . Rose was sweet and tender and maternal, and in all this she was different from everyone else. He could abandon all thought of himself and his troubles while he was with her. It did not matter if he was a hopeless failure as long as she forbore to tell him so.

When she pressed his arm he held her more closely to reassure himself once more, and her kiss brought him peace and comfort.

*C. S. Forester*, The African Queen

Love vanquishes time. To lovers, a moment can be eternity, eternity can be the tick of a clock. Across the barriers of time and the ultimate destiny, love persists, for the home of the beloved, absent or present, is always in the mind and heart. Absence does not diminish love.

*Mary Parrish,* McCalls *magazine*

More than half a century has passed, but I can still remember the exact moment when Rosa the Beautiful entered my life like a distracted angel who stole my soul as she went by. . . . The day I entered her house and was within speaking range of her, I couldn't think of anything to say. I stood there mute, my hat in my hand and my mouth gaping, until her parents, who were well acquainted with such symptoms, came to my rescue. I can't imagine what Rosa could have seen in me ~ or why, with time, she came to accept me as her husband. . . . Her mother explained it to me this way: she said that no one felt strong enough to spend his life protecting her from other men's desire. Many had circled around her, even fallen head over heels in love with her, but until I came along none had made up his mind. Her beauty struck fear into their hearts and they preferred to admire her from afar, not daring to approach her. That had never occurred to me, to tell you the truth.

*Isabel Allende,* The House of the Spirits

# A DEDICATION TO MY WIFE

*To whom I owe the leaping delight*
*That quickens my senses in our wakingtime*
*And the rhythm that governs the repose of our*
*sleepingtime,*
*The breathing in unison.*

*Of lovers whose bodies smell of each other*
*Who think the same thoughts without need of speech*
*And babble the same speech without need of meaning.*

*No peevish winter wind shall chill*
*No sullen tropic sun shall wither*
*The roses in the rose-garden which is ours and ours only*

*But this dedication is for others to read:*
*These are private words addressed to you in public.*

T. S. Eliot

*L*ove does not consist in gazing at each other but in

looking together in the same direction.

*Antoine de Saint-Exupéry*

~ Afterward she remembered the times when she had felt the happiest. The first time was when she and Dick danced together and she felt her beauty sparkling bright against his tall, strong form as they floated, hovering like people in an amusing dream ~ he turned her here and there with such a delicacy of suggestion that she was like a bright bouquet, a piece of precious cloth being displayed before fifty eyes. There was a moment when they were not dancing at all, simply clinging together. Some time in the early morning they were alone, and her damp powdery young body came up close to him in a crush of tired cloth, and stayed there, crushed against a background of other people's hats and wraps . . .

*F. Scott Fitzgerald,* Tender Is the Night

Within a week they were head over heels in love . . . they considered themselves engaged; and they were married in London a week before the beginning of the autumn term. . . .

They had both been so eager, planning a future together; but he had been rather serious about it, even a little awed. . . .

There had followed then a time of such happiness that Chips, remembering it long afterward, hardly believed it could ever have happened before or since in the world. For his marriage was a triumphant success. . . .

But most remarkable of all was the change she made in Chips. . . .

She made him, to all appearances, a new man; though most of the

newness was really a warming to life of things that were old,

imprisoned and unguessed. His eyes gained sparkle; his mind, which

was adequately if not brilliantly equipped, began to move more

adventurously. The one thing he had always had, a sense of humor,

blossomed into a sudden richness to which his years lent maturity.

He began to feel a greater sureness . . .

*James Hilton*, Goodbye, Mr. Chips

A lady of forty-seven who has been married twenty-seven years and has six children knows what love really is and once described it for me like this: "Love is what you've been through with somebody."

*James Thurber*

# Biographies

Joseph Addison (1672–1719), British writer and politician

Mortimer J. Adler (b. 1902), American author and philosopher

Louisa May Alcott (1832–1888), American author

Isabel Allende (b. 1942), Chilean novelist

Honoré de Balzac (1799–1850), French novelist

Pierre-Augustin de Beaumarchais (1732–1799), French dramatist

Sarah Bernhardt (1844–1923), French actress

Elizabeth Bowen (1899–1973), Anglo-Irish novelist

Anne Bradstreet (c. 1612–1672), American poet

Charlotte Brontë (1816–1855), British novelist

e. e. cummings (1894–1962), American poet

Charles Dickens (1812–1870), British novelist

Emily Dickinson (1830–1886), American poet

Alexandre Dumas fils (1824–1895), French novelist and dramatist

Daphne du Maurier (1907–1989), British novelist and short story writer

George Eliot (1819–1880), pen name of Mary Anne Evans, British novelist

T. S. Eliot (1888–1965), American-born British poet, critic, and playwright

Euripides (484–406 B.C.), Greek dramatist and poet

F. Scott Fitzgerald (1896–1940), American novelist and short story writer

C. S. Forester (1899–1966), British novelist

E. M. Forster (1879–1970), British novelist

Kuki Gallmann (b. 1943), Italian writer and conservationist

Kahlil Gibran (1883–1931), Lebanese poet, philosopher, and artist

L. P. Hartley (1895–1972), British author

Helen Hayes (b. 1900), American actress

James Hilton (1900–1954), British novelist and short story writer

Victor Hugo (1802–1885), French author

Martin Luther (1483–1546), German Protestant theologian

Christopher Marlowe (1564–1593), British dramatist

François Mauriac (1885–1970), French novelist, poet, and dramatist

Mistinguette (1873–1956), French dancer, singer

Clement C. Moore (1779–1863), British poet

Mary Parrish (b. 1905), pen name of Margaret Cousins, American writer

Marcel Proust (1871–1922), French novelist

Rainer Maria Rilke (1875–1926), Austrian poet

Antoine de Saint-Exupéry (1900–1944), French novelist, pilot, and journalist

Olive Schreiner (1855–1920), South African novelist

William Shakespeare (1564–1616), British dramatist and poet

Alexander Smith (1830–1867), British poet

Sophocles (496–406 B.C.), Greek dramatist and poet

Elizabeth Taylor (1912–1975), British novelist

Alfred Lord Tennyson (1809–1892), British poet

James Thurber (1894–1961), American humorist and cartoonist

Virgil (70–19 B.C.), Roman poet

Voltaire (1694–1778), French dramatist, philosopher, poet, and novelist

George Whyte-Melville (1821–1878), British author

P. G. Wodehouse (1881–1975), British humorist

W. B. Yeats (1865–1939), Irish poet and playwright